NATURE ICONS SERIES
KINGFISI

MADE IN NORFOLK BY MASCOT MEDIA

FROM THE PUBLISHER OF *WINGS OVER WATER*

Mascot Media Ltd, Granary Barn,
Mill Road, Sutton, Norfolk NR12 9RZ
Tel: 01692 582811
Email: mascot_media@btinternet.com
www.mascotmedia.co.uk

'KINGFISHER'
Published in Great Britain in 2021 by Mascot Media Ltd
This book © Mascot Media
Artwork © various artists, as identified
A CIP catalogue record for this book is available from the British Library.

Alan Marshall has asserted his right under the Copyright, Design and Patents Act, 1988,
to be identified as the author of this book.

SOFTBACK: ISBN: 978-1-9164783-8-1   HARDBACK: ISBN: 978-1-9164783-9-8

Text and book design by Alan Marshall. Edited by Marion Scott Marshall.

Printed by Swallowtail Print, Drayton Industrial Park,
Taverham Road, Drayton, Norwich, Norfolk NR8 6RL
Email: contact@swallowtailprint.co.uk
www.swallowtailprint.co.uk

FSC
www.fsc.org
MIX
Paper from
responsible sources
FSC® C113523

1919900620
Printed on Carbon Captured paper

*In loving memory of my father, Gerald Thomas Marshall (28 August 1929 – 24 December 2020).
Parkinson's disease caused him great distress and discomfort in his final years. A charitable
donation will therefore be made from sales of this book.*

"It was the Rainbow gave thee birth,
And left thee all her lovely hues"

from: The Kingfisher
William Henry Davies (1871–1940)

A TRICK OF THE LIGHT   4-23
KINGFISHER PORTFOLIO   24-165
ARTIST INFORMATION   166-167

CAPTIONS:
Front cover (softback edition) –
Daniel Cole (oil on board) 19cm x 19cm
Title page – Andrew Stock
(watercolour) 18cm x 13cm
Right – Terance James Bond (acrylic)
51cm x 28cm

Back cover (softback), clockwise from
top left – Colin Blanchard (screenprint);
Andrew Haslen (oil on board);
Harriet Mead (sculpture from scrap
metal); Emerson Mayes (oil on paper)

Front cover embossed image
(hardback edition) – Beverley Johnson
(based on linocut p61)

A TRICK OF THE LIGHT

Perhaps Vincent van Gogh got it right. His 1887 oil painting of a small, rather dull bird in sparse vegetation on a river bank bears precious little resemblance to the colour-drenched reproductions found elsewhere in these pages. Yes, this particular bijou bird is French – or at least painted by the artist while in Paris. However, a Continental home isn't responsible for the apparently dowdy plumage he portrays.

'Kingfisher by the Waterside' (1887) – Vincent van Gogh (1853-1890). Oil on canvas, 26.6cm x 19.1cm. Van Gogh Museum, Amsterdam (Vincent van Gogh Foundation)

It is easy to forget that the Kingfisher is an optical illusion. A trick of the light. The bird may be small (the width of this book), but it should be so easy to spot with its coat of many colours. The fact that a hunting male can perch unobtrusively and unnoticed above a slow-moving stream should tell us something about the difference between pigmentation and 'structural coloration'. If the light isn't right, the bird can simply fade from sight.

In art, Kingfishers can sometimes vanish. It took two centuries for one to reappear in John Constable's *The Mill Stream*. Painted seven decades before the Van Gogh, the picture includes the bird with its characteristic blue and red livery, skimming the water near Willy Lott's house.

Constable's Kingfisher was revealed in 2014, after the removal of dirt and discoloured varnish. Another reminder, then, that this bird is sometimes hard to find.

The Kingfisher has always been a challenge for birdwatchers, photographers and artists. Just 16cm in length, fast-moving, sometimes virtually invisible, but recognisable immediately even to those who have never glimpsed one. A brown bird that can appear blue. Like Peacock feathers and numerous butterflies, a master of disguise – hiding in plain sight.

Van Gogh's Kingfisher has its own particular charm, and any dedicated wildlife artist would still have wanted to capture the bird in pencil, paint and ink even if it sported conventional camouflage. The long beak, short tail and striking stubby profile would no doubt appeal. Being small and brown has never been a problem in the bird world.

Less likely, however, would have been the proliferation of bold logos, lurid graphic interpretations and 'chocolate box' depictions resulting from what poet John Clare describes as a "coat of orange, green and blue". Tea towels, crockery, toffee tins and tablemats have long been adorned with bright blue birds. The Kingfisher's image and even name have been borrowed

extensively and abused mercilessly.

This is hardly surprising, as few creatures are quite so decorative. When seen in good light, the male Kingfisher has greenish blue upperparts and a pale azure blue back and rump. There is a red patch by the base of the bill and an ear-patch of the same bright rufous colour. The bird has a green/blue neck stripe, white neck blaze and throat, plus red underparts. The male's black bill has some red at the base, while the female has a black-tipped red lower mandible. In both, the legs and feet are bright red.

From a personal perspective, the Kingfisher is a relatively recent pleasure. My wife and I acquired our first piece of art featuring the bird more than a decade before we ever saw one. A small John Busby (1928-2015) watercolour was among the first pictures in what has become a very large collection of wildlife paintings, prints and sculpture.

Such is the apparent familiarity of this scarce and elusive species that it ranks high among the most popular of British birds, beating the Mute Swan and the Blue Tit, in spite of the fact that most people will only ever see a Kingfisher on the TV or in a book.

When choosing art, British buyers tend to avoid unfamiliar species because they don't visit our gardens or fly over our rooftops.

THE WOOD ENGRAVINGS OF
Agnes Miller Parker

IAN ROGERSON

ERIC ENNION

BIRDS AND SEASONS

BIRDS
AN ARTIST'S VIEW
SELECTED PAINTINGS BY
Terance James Bond

TEXT BY ROB HUME • FOREWORD BY BI

COLLINS BRITISH
BIRDS
Text by John Gooders
Paintings by
Terence Lambert

Kingfishers adorn the covers of numerous art and nature volumes. The artists here are Agnes Miller Parker, Eric Ennion, Terance James Bond and Terence Lambert. All books from the author's private collection

We are happy, however, to delight in this exotic creature that is actually less common in the UK than that gauche invader, the Ring-necked (or Rose-ringed) Parakeet.

Your first Kingfisher sighting is unlikely to disappoint, even if it is a brown blur rather than a bolt of blue. It is a thrill that is slow to fade. Few people tire of these halcyon days. The bird is most often glimpsed flying rapidly, low over water, or hunting fish from riverside perches. They seem occasionally to hover above the water's surface, wings beating frantically.

They can be found in numbers by still or slow-flowing water such as lakes, canals and rivers in lowland areas. While territorial, the mating season and the period immediately after fledging can mean more sightings of pairs and family groups. In winter, some individuals move to estuaries and the coast. As some of us can testify, Kingfishers will visit garden ponds – if of a suitable size.

Fast-moving water holds little appeal. Turbulence is the enemy of the Kingfisher, as it cannot swim, spot its prey or fish easily in such conditions. A secure vantage point where the water is still represents a prime location. From here, the bird's exceptional colour vision and unusual eye positioning make it a fish-spotter extraordinaire. Its beak-heavy physique turns it into a guided missile when plunging for prey.

Clockwise from top left: Thomas Bewick; RB Talbot Kelly; Archibald Thorburn; Donald Watson; Basil Ede; Roland Green; Allen W. Seaby

The birds dine largely on fish, often minnows and sticklebacks, but they will also take aquatic insects, freshwater shrimps and tadpoles to vary their diet. Human anglers shouldn't fear the competition, as Kingfishers prefer their prey to be no more than 25mm in length – although they will occasionally be seen struggling with fish three times that size.

Kingfishers breed in their first year, and the formal process of pairing-up usually begins in February. The courtship is initiated by the male, chasing the female while calling continuously and, later, by ritual feeding. If the male and the female hold neighbouring territory, they may merge and enlarge the home patch for the breeding season.

Seeking a suitable location for nesting, the birds scout for steep sandy banks, preferably free of stones, where they can excavate jointly a nest burrow well clear of the water and perhaps half-a-metre from the top. The site will generally be clear of obstructive vegetation, providing ready access for the fast-moving birds, but limited concealment for approaching predators.

The narrow nest tunnel of around six centimetres in diameter will extend for at least two-thirds of a metre, dipping and widening slightly at the far end to avoid the chance of eggs rolling out. We are talking the bare necessities of life, as the

egg chamber is unlined. It soon becomes malodorous as fish bones and other detritus accumulate. Multiple broods are raised quickly, exploiting optimum conditions and making the most of the nest site.

Typically, the first clutch of six or seven glossy white eggs is laid as March becomes April, with the two adults sharing incubation duties over a 20-day period. Once hatched, the young are very demanding, requiring up to 18 small fish each chick, each day. More than 3,000 successful fishing trips are needed during 24-25 days in order to raise the family, with each chick fed in rotation, shuffling without complaint to the back of the queue to digest and prepare for the next meal. Once out of the nest, the young are fed for just four days before the parents drive them off and start the next brood.

The large family groups spotted in late May disperse quickly. Sadly, the majority of the young perish before they can establish a new territory. Perhaps a quarter of fledglings survive to breed the following year. Kingfishers are not long-lived birds, with few lasting more than one breeding season. The oldest bird on record is thought to have been between seven and eight years of age.

Predation isn't the biggest threat, although cats and rats account for a fair share of fatalities. Lack of food or cold

Kingfisher sequence (Rutland Water) – linocuts by Richard Jarvis (SWLA). Each image 12.5cm x 12.5cm

weather is a far greater danger to Kingfishers young and old. During a severe winter, with ice trapping the food supply, a huge proportion of the Kingfisher population can starve. Late spring and summer floods are almost as damaging in terms of nest destruction and the absence of food.

Man, of course, isn't a bird's best friend. Habitat destruction has long been a contributor to the Kingfisher's decline. Human disturbance of nesting birds is also a serious problem, since broods can fail if something disrupts the feeding routine. The use of machinery to re-grade river banks and drain the adjoining land results each year in the loss of many nests on lowland rivers.

We kill a surprising number with our cars, wreck nests with the wake of speeding boats, and pump rivers full of harmful chemicals and other contaminants. While the era of chronic fertiliser and pesticide run-off is hopefully behind us, spills and poor water management policy still savages the population. The Amber list status of the species owes more to river pollution than to any other cause.

Data from the RSPB and the British Trust for Ornithology (BTO) suggest that the typical summer Kingfisher population

barely exceeds 5,000 pairs, in a range of 3,850-6,400 (2016). It is hardly surprising that most people have never seen the bird, as patience, luck and access to the right location is vital. If you have a supply of suitable fish in your garden, and live close to a natural territory, you might get a visit. Don't dig a pond on the off-chance!

We felt sorry for the Kingfisher that in the summer of 2020 found its way into our garden. The creation of a mighty raised (but so far fish-free) pond during lockdown must have lifted the bird's hopes of an easy meal. After a couple of flypasts, it avoided the glass of our conservatory, settling on to the back of a patio chair before heading elsewhere with better prospects.

They are territorial and do have favourite fishing perches. If you locate a nest site in early April, you stand a good chance of observing the adult birds bringing food and the young emerging. Slow-moving water at river bends with overhanging branches can be a good bet for regular Kingfisher visits. Watching from a little-used bridge over a stream can reap rewards. If you fish, you may well get company. Most anglers are happy to share the waterways with the birds.

When the perched bird has identified a suitable target, and calculated its depth below the surface (ideally less than 25cm), it dives. As it enters the water, the beak is opened and the eyes covered by a transparent third eyelid. The bird rises beak-first from the surface and heads back to its perch – hopefully with a fish on board.

Back on its observation post, the Kingfisher strikes the fish repeatedly against the branch in order to kill it. This not only stops the prey struggling, but causes the spines in the fins to relax – allowing the bird to swallow it head-first. Even when there are no young to worry about, each bird must consume almost its own bodyweight of food every day.

Any bird that cannot secure a territory (of at least 1km) with adequate food supply is likely to perish. This is critical as winter approaches. Kingfishers therefore start to contest territories by mid-September.

Moving to the Norfolk Broads in 2002 was for us the key to becoming Kingfisher confidants, but there were no immediate assignations. The main bodies of water

Field sketches by Paul Henery from two coastal Kingfisher encounters. One was in Amble harbour (Northumberland), the other on a nearby rocky shore

are surprisingly hard to access from the land. Small reclaimed patches at the edge of the shallow man-made lakes were all that was on offer 20 years ago. Short stretches of the linking rivers could (and can) be walked, but the watery paradise remains largely a secret world without a boat.

Infrequent glimpses of perched and flying Kingfishers resulted from regular trips to the periphery of Barton and Hickling Broads, making use of the purpose-made boardwalks. The clumsy outings in our first shabby boat meant closer and more frequent encounters. The rule of thumb tends to be that when your camera is at the ready you'll see nothing. As with the still-more elusive otter, our best sightings are generally when photographic gear is at home or packed away.

Given the area covered by water, you might expect 'wall-to-wall' Kingfishers in the Broads. And, indeed, the population has risen with improved water quality and milder winters. The gently flowing tidal rivers that connect the Broads are very suitable for the birds, but banks are eroded continually by speeding boats. When the Broads ranger tells you to slow down, it isn't just to spoil your fun. The wake from a pleasure boat can do plenty of harm to habitat and wildlife.

Reed bed management and the removal of unplanned trees such as Alder make many stretches of the rivers unsuitable for nest sites, and there may be a lack of perching posts. Kingfishers favour areas with plentiful supplies of small fish and rivers with steep-sided sandy banks suitable for nest hole excavation.

The Broads and the river system are famed for extensive reed beds and, arguably, this is the biggest negative in terms of Kingfisher population growth. This is unlikely to change. More severe tidal events and heavy rains pose a threat. Our

second year as boat owners in the northern Broads saw rising water levels destroy large numbers of spring nests.

The distribution is curious, and reflects a combination of human presence, topography and water quality. We have found the River Ant to be a particularly happy hunting ground for Kingfishers. Our first mooring between Stalham and Hickling, close to Barton Broad, made us almost blasé about the birds. The local staithe itself attracts feathered and human anglers. The dykes and channels are lined with trees and shrubs, while stretches of suitable banking provide homes.

It was therefore possible to see Kingfishers regularly near our mooring and along the route from Sutton towards Barton Broad. In spite of high volumes of holiday boat traffic into and out of Stalham, the nearest stretch of the Ant hosts a good population. An acquaintance occupying a house overlooking the water at Stalham Staithe got very used to a Kingfisher perching on the 'No Mooring' sign beyond her patio.

The charming and peaceful route from Barton towards Wayford Bridge and

Dilham often yields sightings. The North Walsham & Dilham Canal, currently being restored, is known to be a Kingfisher stronghold. Lime Kiln Dyke, linking Barton Broad with Neatishead, provides territories for several birds. Ropes, boats, boathouses and speed signs are used as observation and hunting perches.

From Barton down to the nature reserve at How Hill, Kingfishers can be seen. Excursions on the silent *Electric Eel* through the reed beds can sometimes add to the tally – an *African Queen*-like experience, but with fewer crocodiles and hippos.

When our boat was relocated to Wroxham, in the heart of the tourist Broads, we felt the loss of our Kingfisher sightings. The broader River Bure, playing host to vast numbers of floating pleasure palaces and erratic day boats, is something of a Kingfisher desert. Sightings during our stay were rare, but very welcome. You would have more luck heading up towards Belaugh and Coltishall.

Once past Horning, and heading along the Bure towards St Benet's Abbey and, later, the entrance to the River Thurne, there is more evidence of Kingfishers. Marsh Harrier and otter sightings also increase near South Walsham Broad, Malthouse/Ranworth

'Kingfishers' (1979) – David Koster (1926–2015). Etching, original: 26.6cm x 19.1cm. Private collection

and the nature reserve at Cockshoot.

Autumn and winter are quiet on the waters, but the birds are also seemingly scarce. Spring offers greater opportunity and, while Easter brings the first holiday trade, it remains a good time to pilot a small boat on the Broads network. Public moorings will often have space, unlike during the height of summer – which can be a cross between the M25 in rush hour and a packed supermarket car park.

The River Thurne, south of Potter Heigham bridge, has failed to provide us with many Kingfisher liaisons. Few sandy banks, plenty of reed beds, a plethora of riverside bungalows and a high level of boating activity make it a relatively poor patch for wildlife. Anglers are plentiful, so it is not a lack of fish that is a problem.

Passing, if you can, under the old stone bridge at Potter gives you access to the unspoilt northern reaches of the Thurne. Beyond the chalets are some promising areas of wildlife-friendly water and bank. The slow sail or cruise down to Martham and beyond will provide Kingfisher sightings. Crossing Heigham Sound

towards Hickling and/or Horsey reveals a motherlode of harriers, Bittern, wildfowl and some Kingfisher action.

Our small boat these days nestles alongside the Pleasure Boat Inn at Hickling. The narrow dyke, with stands of nearby trees, attracts the birds that will flit from furled sail to cabin roof, mooring line and mast. The vast body of water that constitutes the biggest of the Broads is now a Norfolk Wildlife Trust (NWT) asset, with nature finally getting priority over the pleasure-seekers.

There is a conservation point to be made here, as much of the work by the over-extended and under-funded Broads Authority may seem to conflict with habitat protection efforts made elsewhere. It can be argued that the Broads aren't being managed solely for nature, but for the holidaymakers, anglers and local boaters who provide much of the funding.

This may seem harsh and, with a foot in both camps, my wife and I acknowledge the conundrum. In many cases, wildlife is benefiting from Broads maintenance and management. The protection and, indeed, restoration of reed beds is helping many bird species, from the warblers up to the Bittern and Marsh Harrier. The poor Kingfisher,

Kingfisher watercolour sketches – Jonathan Pomroy

however, seems to fall between two stools.

As shrubs and trees establish a foothold along the riverbanks, they take the wet out of wetland. Removal at an early stage slows one form of habitat destruction, but halts another form of habitat creation. Wide reed beds extending out into the river and lake edges will not help Kingfishers thrive. Some dredging activity and the removal of piles will displace potential nest sites. No nest holes, and no perching posts, can only mean no Kingfishers.

With the NWT in charge of several key Norfolk wetland sites, dominated by Hickling Broad, it will be fascinating to see if all of the forms of native wildlife can be protected and nurtured, while the often conflicting needs of private and hire boat users are accommodated.

The need to take to the water to appreciate fully the natural wealth of the Broads accounts perhaps for a paucity of local art and artists. Those who like to draw and paint on location will be frustrated by the constraints imposed by boat handling. Stopping mid-stream for even a few minutes to observe and sketch can be life-threatening if a novice-operated

15-metre cruiser is approaching at speed!

Nowadays, there are no big-name artists based in the Broads. Edward Seago (1910-1974) remains the area's most famous artistic son. The late Roland Green (1890-1972) flew the flag for wildlife painters, having made his home on the edge of Hickling Broad – which he used with other Broadland locations as the backdrop for a huge number of artworks. Not surprisingly, the Kingfisher was a regular subject, observed during his endless forays into the reed beds, or from his eyrie atop the disused drainage mill that formed part of his idiosyncratic property.

Wildlife art was born out of illustration, in much the same way that botanical paintings moved from the pages of books to the walls of galleries and homes. Particularly in the era before reliable and affordable photography, illustrators were the only means of bringing nature to the living rooms of the masses.

During the first so-called 'golden age' of wildlife art and illustration, the Kingfisher was an essential part of the portfolio. The birds themselves were by then being killed in smaller numbers for their feathers or as taxidermy specimens. Nonetheless, they were relatively hard to see and study.

Kingfisher field sketches – David Cemmick

Archibald Thorburn (1860-1935) and Charles Tunnicliffe (1901-1979) produced portraits in the classic style, based on years of book illustration. Thorburn may have begun by painting in exquisite detail the creatures that wealthy landowners wished to slaughter, but found his work adopted by and adapted for a more conservation-minded audience. Tunnicliffe illustrated many books with his wood engravings, before becoming the 'house' artist for the RSPB's Christmas cards.

Attitudes to wildlife and nature were changing, and there was gradually less reliance on preserved specimens for bird painting. Twentieth-century artists handy with a gun, such as (Sir) Peter Scott (1909-1989), swapped the Purdey for the pencil and paintbrush. While his art and conservation efforts focused largely on wildfowl, he narrated *The Private Life of the Kingfisher*, the first BBC natural history film to be shown in colour. He and friend Keith Shackleton (1923-2015) had by then eschewed shooting for sketching.

Even in these early days of establishing the wildlife art genre, there were distinctions in approach and result. Not everyone wanted

to paint in minute detail the studio-based recreations favoured by Thorburn, although Basil Ede (1931-2016) carried the baton before passing it to the likes of 1946-born Terance James Bond.

Scott took his flocking birds into a landscape-rich direction, and several followers went with him. R B Talbot Kelly (1896-1971) developed a freedom of line that emphasised movement. Eric Ennion (1900-1981) and John Busby arguably laid the foundations for the more expressive style of wildlife painting that proliferates today. The immediacy of field painting puts the 'wild' back into wildlife art.

The father of wildlife printmaking is arguably Thomas Bewick (1753-1828), although there were limited options for illustrated natural history books in Georgian times. Tunnicliffe was, a century later, responsible for great advances with this ancient technique, joined in nature book illustration by the talented and versatile Agnes Miller Parker (1895-1980).

Printmaking also embraced the influence of colour Japanese woodblocks, thanks to the incomparable Allen W. Seaby (1867-1953). David Koster (1926–2015) brought etching/aquatint and large-scale lithography to the party. Linocutting, in its infancy

Kingfisher woodcut – Allen W. Seaby, original: 15cm x 20cm

during the first golden age, is now an accepted and admired wildlife art technique – thanks in no small part to Seaby's gifted grandson, Robert Gillmor.

In the author's opinion, the result is a new artistic era where ultra-realism meets expressionism, modernism and even the abstract to create a potent cocktail of styles – with a common theme of showcasing nature. Newer materials, tools and techniques have helped improve consistency and increase diversity, at a time when art appreciation is faced with many challenges.

Some of the artists featured in this collection straddle the divide between painting and printmaking, having a recognisable style in both. Robert Greenhalf's painterly woodcuts bear more than a passing resemblance to his oil and watercolour compositions, while Andrew Haslen's bold style and Talbot Kelly influence are present both in his oil paintings and hand-coloured linocuts.

There are black-and-white images in this book. To many, this may seem a wasted opportunity. In a way, it takes us back to Van Gogh's brown bird. The 'right' colours make the subject recognisable to even the

casual observer. Creating an immediately identifiable Kingfisher through incising wood or lino and applying only black ink takes a particular skill.

Of course, Bewick was doing that 200 years ago. His ornithological knowledge could be somewhat patchy, but he inspired generations of printmakers to tackle wildlife subjects with the same tools and materials. We would argue that the likes of Andy English have helped move wildlife wood engraving from mere illustration to a spectacular form of art. Richard Allan produces wonderful work in colour, but has carved his own niche with small, relatively simple black-and-white linocuts that capture attitude as well as the essential detail.

The intention of this book and others in the Mascot Media portfolio is to demonstrate the breadth and depth of talent on our shores, most often dealing with aspects of nature and conservation. Art has a key role to play in education, as well as in entertainment. Hanging a picture on the wall, or placing a sculpture on a table, is an important step towards greater appreciation of the subject, as well as of the artist.

There is work in this book by a breed of artist that has developed, spontaneously, an ability to bring a highly contemporary approach to natural subjects that makes the work not only accessible but desirable in the modern home. Arguably, the classic wildlife art of the first golden age often nowadays

Glazed earthenware tile panel featuring
Kingfishers, dragonflies, frog & lily – Maureen Minchin
(private collection)

struggles to find an appreciative audience.

Ultra-realism still has an important role that hasn't been supplanted by digital photography. To many bird lovers, for example, the feather-by-feather recreations of their favourite species are the greatest form of tribute. When compiling the collection for this book, it would have been entirely possible to fill each page with a perfectly crafted Kingfisher perched serenely above water, sometimes with a fish, often without. Instead, we have selected a variety of artistic approaches, all delivering a recognisable form. It is simply remarkable that a Sparrow-sized brown bird that appears blue can be captured on paper, canvas, board, lino, clay, bronze or even scrap metal in so many ways, without ever missing the essence of the subject.

The 'common' Kingfisher will never become appreciably more widespread; neither will it be easier to spot. Hopefully, the population will at least remain stable, but we cannot afford to be complacent. More of us acknowledge the need to protect the natural environment, but far too few are willing to act on it.

Alan Marshall – Norfolk, March 2021

"One of my favourite visitors is the Kingfisher which comes regularly to help itself to some of the small rudd that inhabit my pond. A flash of blue or mouse-like squeak gets me grabbing my binoculars or telescope to get a better view. It is a bird I have drawn many times over the years. I am attracted to its bold electric colours and the clearly defined patterns of its plumage" Andrew Haslen

Right: 'Minsmere Kingfisher'
– Andrew Haslen (SWLA)
Oil on board
30cm x 30cm

Left: 'Kingfisher at Sunset'
– Andrew Haslen
Hand-coloured linocut
32cm x 32cm
Edition of 25

"It is always a pleasure to see a Kingfisher, even if it is only a glimpse of a blue streak beside the water. There is a tributary of the River Cam where I would see one regularly and, since I like to engrave a bird in a real setting, I engraved 'Kingfisher At Bourn Brook' with a favourite group of trees in the background"

Andy English

'Kingfisher at Bourn Brook' – Andy English (SWE)
Wood engraving
Original image: 14.8cm x 11.5cm
Edition of 100

"Some paintings have the capacity to evoke certain memories, and this image of a Kingfisher is one such. The location was the out-stream of the huge dam at Nant-y-Moch Reservoir, a wonderful place high in the mountains, south of the Snowdon range"

Terance James Bond

'Kingfisher on Stone' ~ Terance James Bond
Acrylic on board
Original image: 42cm x 30cm

"She saw a Kingfisher darting blue – and then she was very happy"

from *The Rainbow*, by D H Lawrence

Daniel Cole (SWLA)
Oil on board
19cm x 19cm

KINGFISHER

"I aim to capture movement & personality – the inner
life of subjects I choose. I often focus in on close images
of head and rely on the eye, the look, the stare to bring
the animal to life in the print. The challenge here was the
colours – the essence and glory of a Kingfisher.
After eventually abandoning my blue and orange blocks,
I used drawing inks to hand-finish the blue
and orange sections"

David Gilbert

David Gilbert
Linocut
20cm x 15cm
Edition of 12

*The modern binomial name derives from the Latin **Alcedo**,*
*Kingfisher (from Greek **halcyon**), and **Atthis**, a beautiful young*
woman from the island of Lesbos, and favourite of Sappho

Main image – Brin Edwards (SWLA)
Oil on canvas
Original image: 12.5cm x 12.0cm

"Never seen one! Something I commonly hear from people when I mention Kingfishers. They can be unobtrusive, surprisingly small, dark and motionless when fishing. Then there's a splash, and a flash of orange and azure streaks past carrying a silver shard in its bill"

Richard Allen

*Main image
– Richard Allen (SWLA)
Linocut (from 'Coastal Birds')
12.5cm x 12.5cm*

*Left, by the same artist,
watercolour sketch from
Abberton Reservoir (Essex).
Kingfisher perched in glorious
afternoon sun*

KINGFISHER

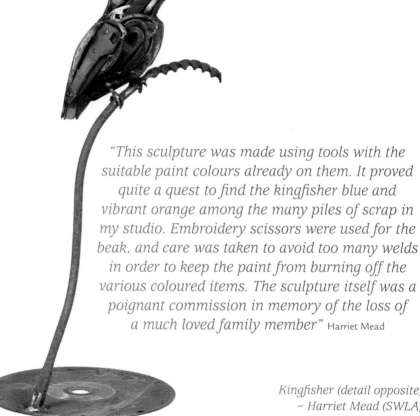

"This sculpture was made using tools with the suitable paint colours already on them. It proved quite a quest to find the kingfisher blue and vibrant orange among the many piles of scrap in my studio. Embroidery scissors were used for the beak, and care was taken to avoid too many welds in order to keep the paint from burning off the various coloured items. The sculpture itself was a poignant commission in memory of the loss of a much loved family member" Harriet Mead

Kingfisher (detail opposite)
– Harriet Mead (SWLA)
Sculpture from scrap metal

"I always think that the Kingfisher adds a touch of the exotic to the British landscape – can there be a more colourful bird? Notoriously difficult to watch and study, they are seen most commonly as a blue streak along the water course. When they do perch long enough to set my telescope on, it is as if someone has taken the brightest summer sky to illuminate the view. Unbeatable!"

Darren Rees

Darren Rees (SWLA)
Watercolour on Saunders paper
Original image: 31cm x 23cm

"Unlike 'Fisherman' [page 143], 'Catch' was a more immediate print and made entirely by hand painting screen-blocking fluid directly on to the screenprint mesh to make the stencils. With care, very dilute layers of this fluid can be made to only partially block the mesh, giving a watercolour or half-tone effect"

Colin Blanchard

'Catch' – Colin Blanchard
Screenprint
22cm x 22cm

KINGFISHER

↑ *Pages 46-47: 'Winter Kingfisher'*
– Andrew Haslen
Oil on canvas
Original image: 46cm x 61cm

"How thrilling is the moment, when standing on a river bank, to notice that unmistakable flash of electric blue. These gorgeous birds are made all the more charming by their almost mythical transience. Their unique plumage makes them an artist's dream to depict, but to capture their true iridescence is a lifetime's work"

Shelly Perkins

'Kingfishers' Courtship' – Shelly Perkins
Multi-layered digital collage print
45cm x 45cm

Paul Henery
Watercolour sketches

"Pushed to the windswept North Sea coast by winter's bite, the Kingfisher perches on a frayed rope unnoticed amongst the hulking trawlers and rusting ladders on the harbour wall, a ripple breaking the boat reflections the only sign of its passing"

Paul Henery

'The Harbour Wall' – Paul Henery
Watercolour
Original image: 37cm x 57cm

"'Kingfisher!' is my usual reaction as I hear the high-pitched whistle followed by a flash of blue as it shoots past. On this occasion I was beside one of the slow-flowing drainage dykes on Pevensey Levels, Sussex, admiring the late summer marsh vegetation when the bird came – and was gone in a second"

Robert Greenhalf

'Kingfisher!' –
Robert Greenhalf (SWLA)
Multi-block woodcut
24cm x 29cm
Edition of 100

*Slow-moving water at river
bends with overhanging
branches can be a good bet for
regular Kingfisher visits*

*Right: Brin Edwards
Acrylic on canvas
20cm x 20cm*

*Left: Brin Edwards
Acrylic on board
25cm x 13cm*

"The note of the Kingfisher is a clear
whistling cry, several times repeated.
The flight is straight and rapid, usually
carried out close to the water…"

British Birds volume II, Archibald Thorburn

'Willow Bank' – Annie Soudain
Reduction linocut
30cm x 30cm

"I was watching and sketching the bird on the right while it perched on a swaying reed. The Kingfisher has the astonishing ability to stabilise its head and keep its eyes focused on its prey"

Peter Partington

Main image: 'Among the Water Mint'
– Peter Partington (SWLA)
Watercolour
Original image: 30cm x 21cm
Sketches above right by same artist

"Azure fisher king
Black eyes, a flash of feathers
A sudden bold dive"

Beverley Johnson

"I wanted my image to portray the beauty and grace of the
extraordinary Kingfisher. For that reason I have purposely
left the space around my fisher king spare so as not to detract
from his magnificence"

Beverley Johnson

'The Fisher King' – Beverley Johnson
Linocut
15cm x 15cm

↑ *Pages 62-63: 'Kingfisher in Stream' – Terance James Bond*
Acrylic on board
Original image:
46cm x 61cm

"From the Bure Valley in the Norfolk village of Buxton with Lamas. For such brightly coloured birds, they can be surprisingly unobtrusive. I found this one deep in the shadows of a weeping willow, lit by the reflections of the stream below"

Johnnie Foker

←
Main image – Johnnie Foker (SWLA)
Oil on board
15cm x 18cm

"*The main print features a Kingfisher perched on a willow branch
amidst reed mace and irises by Aylsham water mill in Norfolk.
'Riverside' was inspired by a leisurely rowing boat trip on the
River Great Ouse at Houghton Mill in Cambridgeshire*"

Kate Heiss

"As Kingfishers catch fire, dragonflies draw flames"

Gerard Manley Hopkins

Daniel Cole
Oil on board
19cm x 19cm

KINGFISHER

"When designing this image, the intention was not to use any outlining, so one element ends and another starts with no boundary line. Such a minor detail to the observer, but a challenging undertaking for the artist"

Andrew Stock

'Kingfisher' – Andrew Stock (SWLA)
Hand-coloured etching
10cm x 10cm

Pages 72-73: 'Passing Kingfisher' ↑
– Andrew Haslen
Oil on canvas
Original image: 46cm x 61cm

"During the winter months we are very
privileged to receive visits to our garden pond
and moat by these incredibly attractive birds"

Paul Evans

→
'Kingfisher Colours on a Grey Day' – Paul Evans
Ink and gouache
28cm x 28cm

*Left: original
watercolour painting
(20cm x 15cm) by
Katharine Green for
main image*

*Katharine Green
Hand-coloured linocut
Original image:
20cm x 15cm*

KINGFISHER

"These field sketches were made from direct observation at a nest I knew in County Durham"

David Cemmick

'The Fisher King' – David Cemmick
Hand-coloured bronze sculpture
Edition of 12
Detail on facing page

Pages 80-81: 'Canalside Kingfisher'
– Richard Jarvis (SWLA)
Hand-tinted linocut
Original image: 20cm x 31cm
Edition of 20

"'Canalside Kingfisher' was produced in February 2020 after a particularly close encounter with a female Kingfisher along the canal. It allowed some quick sketches to be made, and the resulting print reproduced the encounter. The bird perched amongst the hips of the wild rose"

Richard Jarvis

The Kingfisher has no song. The flight call is a short, sharp whistle 'chee' repeated two or three times...

→

Main image: 'Red Shoes'
– Sarah Cemmick
Linocut/watercolour
15cm x 15cm

"*This tiny, exquisitely coloured, aquatic British bird really comes to its iridescent best when it catches the sunlight as it darts upon some watery fishing quest*"

Barrie Morris

'Cutting a Dash' ~ Barrie Morris
Mixed media
40cm x 50cm

KINGFISHER

"Here, the Kingfisher competes with the hues of the season as October's confetti tumbles downstream – the bird resting between dives upon the stream's sub-surface residents. Inspired by the work of the pre-Raphaelites Millais and Waterhouse, I painted this large canvas quickly over two days. Any longer and I feel that any freshness in the brushstrokes would have been lost"

David Cowdry

'Autumn Cascade' – David Cowdry
Acrylic on canvas
Original image: 102cm x 76cm

"You rarely 'see' a Kingfisher. It's mostly a 'glimpse'.
I live on a creek in Kent and the resident Kingfisher is often
present but typically elusive in and around the moored boats
on the waterfront as he fishes"

Hugh Ribbans

'The Catch' – Hugh Ribbans
5-block linocut
13cm x 13cm
Edition of 20

KINGFISHER

Pages 90-91: 'Kingfisher, Lyme Regis harbour' – Andrew Stock
Oil on paper
Original image: 56cm x 76cm

"This bird was sketched from a hide at Rutland Water where it perched and fished for some time on a bright October day"

Richard Jarvis

Main image: 'Autumn Kingfisher'
– Richard Jarvis
Hand-tinted linocut
12.5cm x 12.5cm
Edition of 30

"In coat of orange, green, and blue
Now on a willow branch I view"

John Clare

'Sitting on the Stump' – Catriona Hall
Acrylic on board
30cm x 30cm

KINGFISHER

"This small linocut was inspired by sightings of a Kingfisher flying low over marshland, appearing suddenly and then disappearing into a Great Sallow tree. The Sallow, or Goat Willow, is a favourite roosting site and a safe place for the bird to digest its most recent meal"

Michael Webb

'Kingfisher in the Sallow' – Michael Webb
Linocut
14.5cm x 12.8cm

"What makes the Kingfisher so special? The fact that it is this country's most brightly coloured bird often comes second in my mind to that sense of anticipation I so often feel when near water. Even with my eyes constantly scanning the riverbank, a quick blink and I can miss the bright blue 'torpedo' dart by – with often only its shrill whistle to let me know I've missed it"

Emerson Mayes

'Study of a Kingfisher'
– Emerson Mayes
Oil on paper
Original image: 42cm x 34cm

*The common Kingfisher was first described by
Carl Linnaeus in the 10th edition of his
Systema Naturae published in 1758*

*'Kingfisher' – Robert Greenhalf
Hand-coloured woodcut
Original image: 24cm x 22cm*

'Juvenile Kingfishers'
– Peter Partington
Watercolour from sketchbook
15cm x 21cm

"We were saying goodbye
to some birdwatching
friends when I noticed
what I thought was a
discarded blue crisp bag
in the pond vegetation
across the drive. I gasped
when my binoculars
revealed not litter, but a
family of Kingfishers. The
birds stayed for a day or
two and individuals spent
some time with us
that summer"

Peter Partington

Main image: 'Kingfisher Family' – Peter Partington
Oil
Original image: 58cm x 38cm

Both paintings oil on canvas – Andrew Haslen
Above: 'Out of the Light'
40cm x 50cm
Right: 'Winter Kingfisher II'
40cm x 40cm

KINGFISHER

*"My linocut aims to capture the movement of the bird's dive –
the swirl and displacement of the water"*

Rebecca Perdue

Rebecca Perdue
Linocut
15cm x 15cm

KINGFISHER

*"These old fishing nets and ropes in Southwold caught my attention –
I was drawn to the arrangement of colours and textures. As a subject,
the Kingfisher was the obvious choice. The colours of the bird and the
association with boats and water seemed perfect"*

Terance James Bond

*'Kingfisher on Nets and Rope' – Terance James Bond
Acrylic on board
Original image: 76cm x 46cm*

KINGFISHER

"Long of beak and short of tail
Jewelled plumage reflects the light
A streak, a blur, a fleeting glimpse
Then vanished, out of sight"

Anon

Julie Orpen
Reduction linocut
12.5cm x 12.0cm

KINGFISHER

↑ Pages 112-113: 'The Kingfishers of Peckham Rye' – Sanchia Lewis Oil paintings on Meridian high-density board, acid-free and buffered. Each 25.5cm x 25.5cm

"On an early morning walk in Peckham Rye Park, we reached the Japanese Gardens and followed a path next to the stream. As we passed the Japanese rain shelter, a small blue and orange bird whisked by, flew under the bridge and disappeared. A Kingfisher – we were thrilled! Whenever I walk through the Japanese Gardens I look at the bridge hoping for another sighting..."

Sanchia Lewis

→
'The Dive' – Hugh Ribbans Hand-coloured linocut 13.5cm x 13.3cm Edition of 20

KINGFISHER

"If I am lucky when walking along the bank of the River Rib I see the brilliant blue flash of the Kingfisher. This relief solarplate was produced from my drawing, and my hand-decorated tissue was used as chine-collé to capture the brilliance of colour"

Janet Gardner

'Kingfisher' – Janet Gardner
Relief print with decorated
chine-collé tissue
Original image: 14cm x 20cm

KINGFISHER

When seen in good light, the male Kingfisher has greenish blue upperparts and a pale azure blue back and rump. There is a red patch by the base of the bill and an ear-patch of the same bright rufous colour

'The Fisher King'
– Catriona Hall
Acrylic on board
30cm x 30cm

"A painting made from a visit to the Bure Valley in the Norfolk village of Buxton with Lamas. I love this stretch of river, and there's a footbridge that gave me the vantage point for 'Blue Streak'"

Johnnie Foker

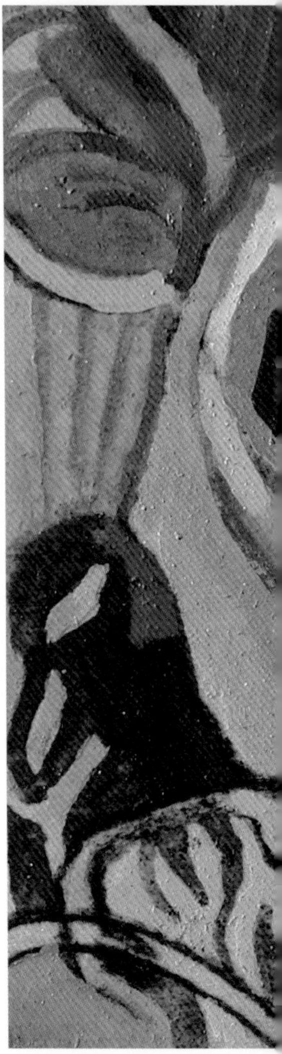

'Blue Streak' – Johnnie Foker
Oil on board
15cm x 18cm

"Kingfishers are often thought of as birds of the inland waterways; birds that frequent only the streams, rivers and lakes of freshwater. This is not always so. Many times I have enjoyed their company during my coastal wanderings. Even a mile out to sea, bobbing about in my kayak, I've enjoyed the blue flash fly-by of a Kingfisher"

David Cowdry

'Coastal Kingfisher, Last Light' – David Cowdry
Oil on board
68cm x 64cm

"Driven by the cold and ice, the winter Kingfisher haunts the rocky shore of the windswept Northumberland coast. A tropical jewel of azure and orange perching to preen and stretch among limpets, barnacles and bladderwrack. This tiny gem plummets in a shower of spray into a crystal-clear rockpool before rising once again, fish firmly grasped in its dagger beak"

Paul Henery

'Kingfisher on the Rocky Shore'
– Paul Henery
Watercolour
Original image: 27cm x 37cm

KINGFISHER

*One's first Kingfisher sighting is unlikely to disappoint,
even if it is a brown blur rather than a bolt of blue.
It is a thrill that is slow to fade...*

*Main image: 'King fisher'
– Anne Townshend
Reduction linocut
20cm x 20cm*

*Right: 'Skyfall'
– Anne Townshend
Reduction linocut
11cm x 20cm*

It is easy to forget that the Kingfisher is an optical illusion.
A trick of the light. The bird may be small, but it should be
so easy to spot with its coat of many colours

'Kingfisher, August Morning' –
Emerson Mayes
Oil on paper
Original image: 44cm x 46cm

KINGFISHER

*"A swift flicker of turquoise and orange across your vision is
the moment when you realise you've just seen a Kingfisher.
That's been my experience: a briefly glimpsed arrow of
colour, then it's gone"*

Ann Bridges

*'K is for Kingfisher'
– Ann Bridges
Stencil-based monoprint
Both versions: 20cm x 20cm*

KINGFISHER

"The freeze on my local waterways has forced the Kingfishers to hunt any small patches of open water. If the icy temperatures aren't enough to contend with, the murky waters draining from the fields cloud the bird's sight of any available prey. These factors, combined with the flattened winter vegetation, allow great views of this stunning little bird"

David Bennett

'Kingfisher and Hogweed' – David Bennett (SWLA)
Watercolour on paper
34cm x 51cm

The Kingfisher is most often glimpsed flying
rapidly, low over water, or hunting fish
from riverside perches

'A Flash of Blue' – Chris Sinden (SWLA)
29-block linocut
11cm x 27cm
Edition of 25

'Family Outing' – Jackie Cox
Painting on silk
38cm x 14cm

English: Kingfisher
Scottish Gaelic: Biorra-crùidein
Welsh: Glas y Dorlan
Irish: Cruidín

Artwork for Royal Mail Post & Go
British Birds III (2011) – Robert Gillmor
Linocut
Original image: 20.5cm x 26.5cm

"I have only seen a Kingfisher twice in my life: once in a London park and once by a river in Edinburgh. Both sightings elicited a shock of pleasure, as the pop of the unmistakable iridescent colour shone out from the shadowy undergrowth. The Kingfisher for me is a rare and elusive prize. A tiny waterside gem"

Amanda Ribbans

'Pop' – Amanda Ribbans
Three-colour linocut, printed on Japanese Hosho paper
15cm x 15cm

"Do you think that fish see in colour?
Surely they cannot he thought.
But he didn't see you either
Like so many times before.

Until one day – did you decide?
That the boy was righteous enough.
And your straight line spark down the river
Shocked a blue into his eye for life"

Colin Blanchard

"This is quite a complex print that began with separate
linocut images of the bird and the fish. I like the discipline of
line that lino insists on – images have a strength and quality
very different to drawing or painting. The single colour images
were scanned, manipulated and composed to make a photo
stencil screen print. This, in turn, was overprinted with further
hand-painted screen stencils using blends of transparent ink"

Colin Blanchard

'Fisherman' – Colin Blanchard
Screenprint and linocut
40cm x 23cm
Edition size: 15

"This splendid little bird is of rather a clumsy shape, the head being large in proportion to the size of the body, and the legs and feet very small. The middle of the back, the rump, and coverts of the tail are of a most resplendent azure"

Bewick's British Birds

Pam Grimmond
Linocut
18cm x 28cm
Edition of 30

KINGFISHER

"Winter on the canal is a good time to see Kingfishers as reedbed management means areas are cleared, providing excellent vantage points"

David Bennett

"This Kingfisher captures the bright and vibrant colours of this spectacular British bird resting on the bough of a tree overlooking a pond. It's only a brief moment before it's gone"

Sharon Curtis

$\rightarrow$
Sharon Curtis
7-colour reduction linocut
Edition of 5
28.5cm x 28.5cm

Pages 150-151: 'Winter Jewel'
– David Miller
Oil on board
Original image: 41cm x 61cm

"On my way to and from my studio I pass by a small pond where, if I'm lucky, I'll spot the Kingfishers. 'Diving' is an imagined piece inspired by their near constant activity during the summer"

Jackie Cox

"I like the fact that the Kingfisher is not only glorious, but also a fugitive bird. More often than not, I see only a blue flash along a stream. If lucky enough to see one sitting, it is so intent on looking for fish that we can watch it at leisure. I have engraved two birds in two different locations. Bourn Brook is a tributary of the River Cam, and 'Kingfisher Watching' is located beside a drainage channel just 10 minutes' walk from the studio. 'Kingfisher Diving' tries to capture

'Kingfisher Watching' – Andy English
Wood engraving
9cm x 5cm

that moment just before it enters the water to catch a fish. A black and white wood engraving might seem a strange way to portray this most colourful bird, but almost everything I do is monochrome, concentrating on light and form rather than colour. However, I often engrave from an ink drawing washed with watercolours, and I am always conscious of the colour while I make my marks. We all have our approaches to printmaking, and this is mine"

Andy English

'Kingfisher Diving' – Andy English
Wood engraving
9cm x 5cm

↑ *Pages 156-157:*
'Kingfisher, August Rain'
– Emerson Mayes
Oil on paper
Original image: 45cm x 60cm

"As a child I remember being taken Chub fishing by my Dad on the upper reaches of the River Rother in Sussex. The steep-banked river ran through hopfields on one side and rough woodland on the other. The glimpse of a Kingfisher heading upstream always made my day..."

Chris Sinden

←
'Kingfisher' – Chris Sinden
Linocut
9cm x 18cm
Edition of 28

KINGFISHER

159

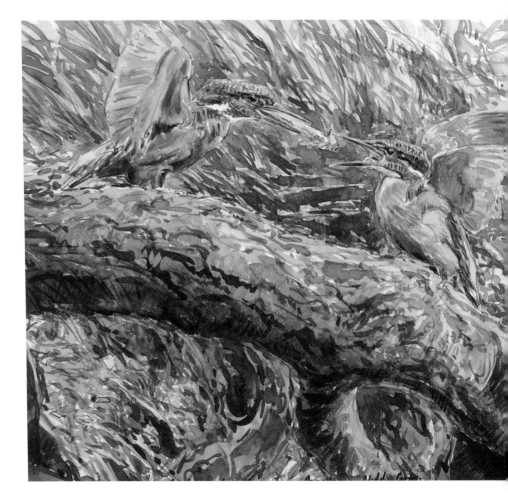

KINGFISHER

↑   *Pages 160-161: 'Kingfisher Family, Nidd Gorge' &*
'Kingfisher Sat in Alder'– David Bennett
Watercolour on paper. 36cm x 53cm, 52cm x 34cm

"Water levels in the Gorge fluctuate greatly during the summer depending on the rainfall on the surrounding moors. These Kingfishers nested just above the waterline – but, thankfully, a good summer meant the nest stayed dry and the young fledged successfully"

"The most abundant tree along the canal is the alder. Happy to have its roots submerged, its boughs reach out into open water making excellent perches for hunting Kingfishers"

David Bennett

→
'Halcyon' – Vanna Bartlett
Linocut
12cm x 12cm
Edition of 15

KINGFISHER

Right: 'The Fisherman' – David Miller
Oil on board
30cm x 30cm

Left: 'Kingfisher Bank'
– David Miller
Oil on paper
30cm x 20cm

Human anglers shouldn't fear the competition, as Kingfishers prefer their prey to be no more than 25mm in length

DAVID MILLER 05

ARTIST INFORMATION

Allen, Richard (SWLA)   *www.richardallenillustrator.com*
Essex-based wildlife artist who loves painting birds in the field & producing distinctive monochrome linocut prints

Bartlett, Vanna   *www.vanna-art.co.uk*
Norwich artist & invertebrate enthusiast who draws, paints & makes linocut prints nowadays favouring insects & spiders

Bennett, David (SWLA)   *www.davidbennettwildlifeart.com*
Yorkshire wildlife artist employing field observations and working with watercolour, acrylic & oil

Blanchard, Colin   *www.colinblanchard.com*
Lockerbie-based artist working most recently in linocut & screenprint with a wildlife theme & the occasional poem

Bond, Terance James   *email bond.art@btconnect.com*
Suffolk painter specialising in life-size, highly detailed bird depictions, generally in acrylic on board

Bridges, Ann   *www.ann-bridges.com*
Kent-based artist who enjoys observational drawing that provides the basis for small-edition original prints

Cemmick, David   *www.davidcemmickart.co.uk*
Cumbrian artist & nature enthusiast producing bronze wildlife sculptures, paintings and field sketches

Cemmick, Sarah   *www.sarahcemmicklinocuts.com*
Based with husband David in Cumbria, Sarah specialises in hand-tinted animal-themed linocuts

Cole, Daniel (SWLA)   *email danielcole5@hotmail.co.uk*
A highly recognisable style using largely oil on board provides striking landscapes and vivid bird studies

Cowdry, David   *@davidcowdryart (Instagram)*
Based in Wales, David emphasises light & atmosphere in his predominantly oil paintings of wildlife and landscape

Cox, Jackie   *www.sindencox-art.co.uk*
A versatile artist based in the Forest of Dean, Jackie is a signature member of the UK Coloured Pencil Society

Curtis, Sharon   *www.artbysharon.co.uk*
Professional artist based in Ross-on-Wye & specialising in reduction linocuts & Kirigami paper art

Edwards, Brin (SWLA)   *www.brin-edwards.com*
Suffolk-based wildlife artist working predominantly in oils & interpreting the effects of light on largely avian subjects

English, Andy (SWE)   *www.andyenglish.com*
Multi-faceted Ely-based wood engraver with a love of landscape & the natural world

Evans, Paul   *www.paulevans-artist.co.uk*
Suffolk-based landscape artist working in watercolour, inks & acrylic, often with East Anglian inspiration

Foker, John (SWLA)   *www.bearparkartists.co.uk*
Based in Durham, Johnnie is a distinctive painter/printmaker emphasising environment as well as birdlife

Gardner, Janet   *email janet.a.gardner@gmail.com*
Hertfordshire-based printmaker who currently specialises in linocutting, drypoint & solar plate printing

Gilbert, David   *etsy.com/shop/wildlinobydave*
Retired teacher turned printmaker who is transforming a love of wildlife into increasingly accomplished linocut prints

Gillmor, Robert (SWLA)   *www.pinkfootgallery.co.uk*
A founder of the SWLA and veteran wildlife artist based in Norfolk and specialising in highly individual printmaking

Green, Katharine   *www.katharinegreen.com*
Herts-based printmaker using strong colours and hand-painting to produce flora- and fauna-themed linocuts

Greenhalf, Robert (SWLA)   *www.robertgreenhalf.co.uk*
A Sussex-based wildlife painter & printmaker whose colourful woodcuts complement his oils & watercolours

Grimmond, Pam   *www.pamgrimmond.co.uk*
Pam's striking wildlife-oriented linocuts reflect the landscape & nature of her North Yorkshire home

Hall, Catriona   *www.catrionahall.com*
The Peak District landscape provides both inspiration & the backdrop to the artist's colourful paintings of birds & beasts

Haslen, Andrew (SWLA)   *www.andrewhaslen.com*
Suffolk artist currently focusing on bold oil paintings of birds & mammals, adding to his earlier linocut-based portfolio